# GETTING TO KNOW THE NATIVE AMERICAN INDIAN TRIBES

## US HISTORY FOR KIDS
## CHILDREN'S AMERICAN HISTORY

Speedy Publishing LLC

40 E. Main St. #1156

Newark, DE 19711

www.speedypublishing.com

Copyright 2017

All Rights reserved. No part of this book may be reproduced or used in any way or form or by any means whether electronic or mechanical, this means that you cannot record or photocopy any material ideas or tips that are provided in this book.

Were all Native American tribes the same? If not, how are they different? Let's visit some great Native American tribes and find out.

# A LAND OF MANY PEOPLES

Before the Europeans arrived in North America, millions of people lived on the continent. They were members of hundreds of tribes, and those tribes were connected with each other. Sometimes they were bitter enemies, but most of the time they traded with each other, joined together to hunt or to fight a common enemy, and shared a world view and many spiritual rituals.

To learn more about Native American spirituality, read the Baby Professor book The World is Full of Spirits: Native American Indian Religion, Mythology and Legends.

Here are introductions to seven of the great Native American tribes.

# NAVAJO

The tribe we call "Navajo" calls itself "Dine", which means "The People". They live in the southwestern United States, in what is now Arizona, New Mexico, Colorado, and Utah. Theirs is the largest Indian reservation in the United States. Learn about these areas, reserved for Native Americans, in the Baby Professor book Are Indian Reservations Part of the US?

MEMBERS OF THE ALAMO NAVAJO RESERVATION

The Navajo lived in hogans, houses made with a wooden frame and clay walls. The door of each hogan faces the rising sun.

Navajo people traditionally were farmers, raising corn, beans, and squash. After the Europeans arrived, the tribe began herding sheep and goats. Hunters also went out after game ranging from deer to prairie dogs.

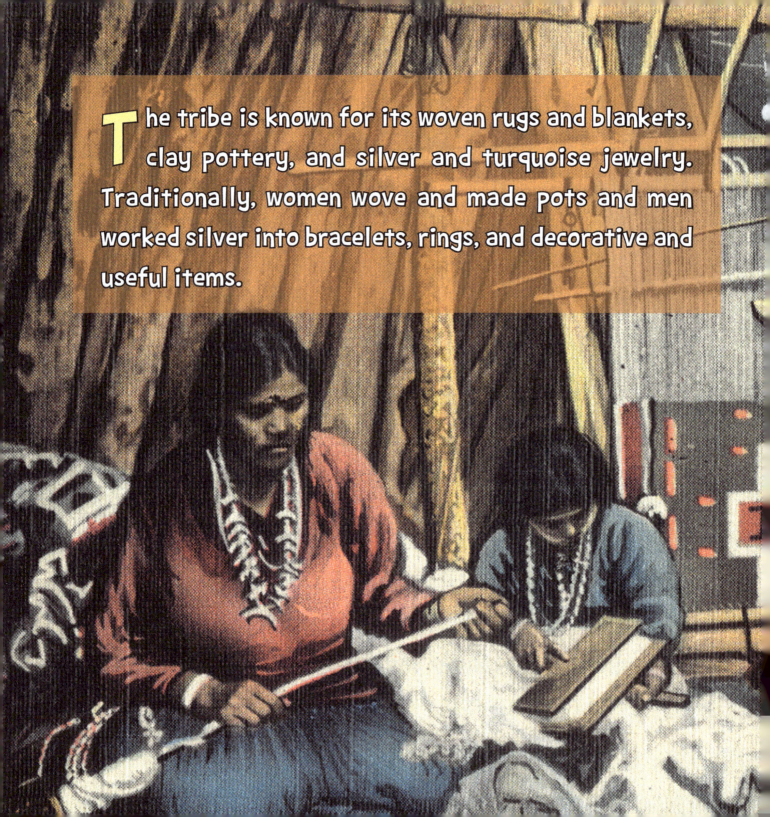

The tribe is known for its woven rugs and blankets, clay pottery, and silver and turquoise jewelry. Traditionally, women wove and made pots and men worked silver into bracelets, rings, and decorative and useful items.

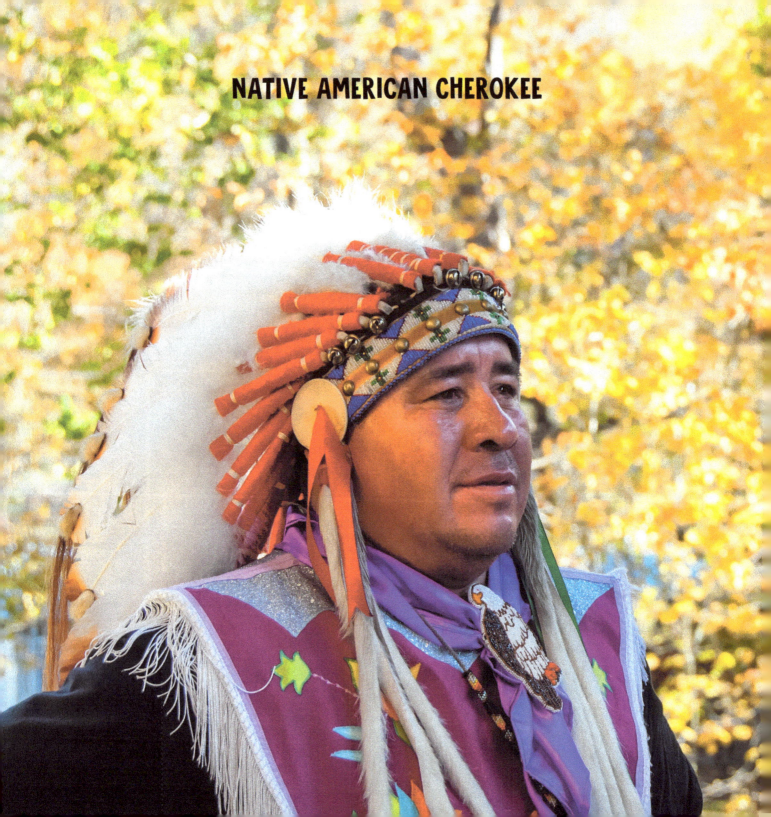

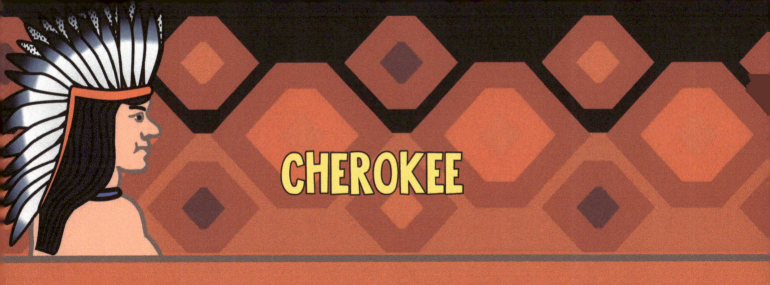

# CHEROKEE

The Cherokee lived in the southeast of North America, in what is now North and South Carolina, Georgia, Alabama, and Tennessee. They lived in homes made of "wattle and daub": the building had a wooden frame with walls made of light branches, grass, and mud. "Cherokee" is a word from another tribe that means "the people who speak that other language". The Cherokee call themselves "ani-yunwiya", or "the main people".

Farming and hunting provided food for the Cherokee, and their diet included both crops like corn and squash and meat from rabbits, turkeys, and deer. They hunted on foot, or using canoes made of hollowed-out logs.

CORN

Cherokee villages had between thirty and fifty families. They farmed and hunted, and marked all important life occasions with ceremonies and prayers to the spirits. Their greatest annual event was the Green Corn Ceremony, thanking the spirits for the harvest.

The Cherokee were good fighters. They sided with the French in the French and Indian Wars. When the British won, they punished the Cherokee by taking away a lot of their traditional land. They lost more land when they fought on the British side against the colonists in the American Revolution.

THE INDIAN CHIEF
A GREAT WARRIOR OF THE CHEROKEE NATION

TRAIL OF TEARS

In 1835, the Cherokee sold what was left of their traditional land to the U.S. government. They were forced to walk to other land in Oklahoma, and over four thousand Cherokee died during the journey. Read the Baby Professor book The Heart-Shattering Facts about the Trail of Tears to learn more about this sad event.

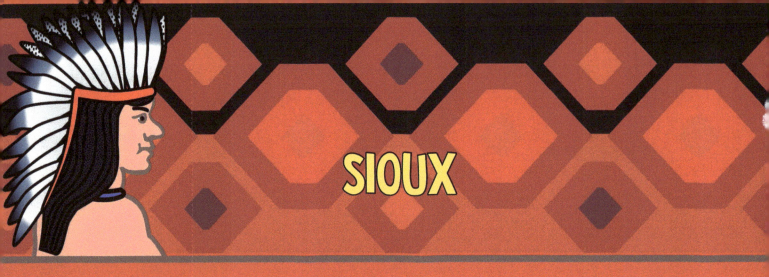

# SIOUX

The Sioux Nation is a group of related tribes who made their home in the great plains of the United States and Canada. Many of the tribes were mainly hunters, constantly on the move as they followed herds of buffalo and other game. They lived in teepees, tents that could be put up and taken down again quickly.

Some Sioux tribes raised or traded for corn, beans and squash, but most of their food was what they could hunt or trap. They killed and ate buffalo, deer,

and other animals. They would dry a lot of the meat from each kill into jerky, a leathery substance that could last a long time without refrigeration.

Sioux life, work, legends, and location all depended on the buffalo. They used every part of each animal: the meat for food, the sinews for bow strings and for tying things, and the skins as walls of their teepees and material for clothing. They carved tools and utensils from buffalo bones.

SIOUX BUFFALO HORN LADDLE

BUFFALO HUNTING

Before they had horses, the Sioux hunted the buffalo on foot. Sometimes they would try to get a whole herd running toward a cliff edge: some of the buffalo would fall over the cliff and be hurt or die, and then the hunters could climb down and deal with them. Once they had horses, the Sioux became masters at hunting and fighting from horseback.

# CHIPPEWA

The Chippewa are also called the Ojibway, a word that means "puckered" in Algonquian and which refers to the rippled edges of typical Chippewa moccasins. The tribe calls itself "Anishinabe", which means "the very first people".

OJIBWA

CHIPPEWA

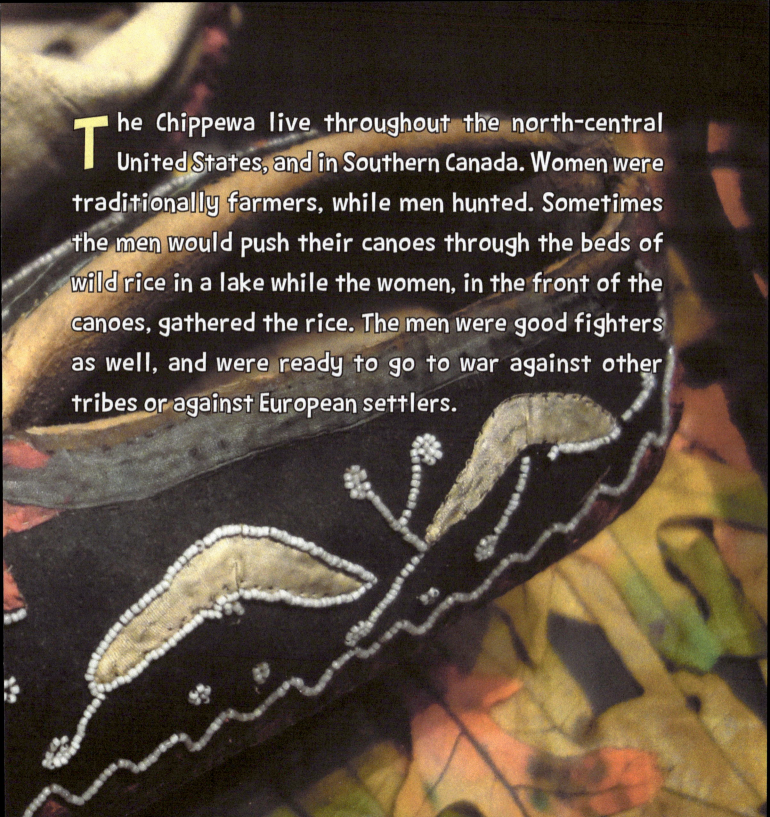

The Chippewa live throughout the north-central United States, and in Southern Canada. Women were traditionally farmers, while men hunted. Sometimes the men would push their canoes through the beds of wild rice in a lake while the women, in the front of the canoes, gathered the rice. The men were good fighters as well, and were ready to go to war against other tribes or against European settlers.

An Ojibway village in wooded areas was made of "waginogans", houses made of birch bark and poles. In the plains, they lived in teepees.

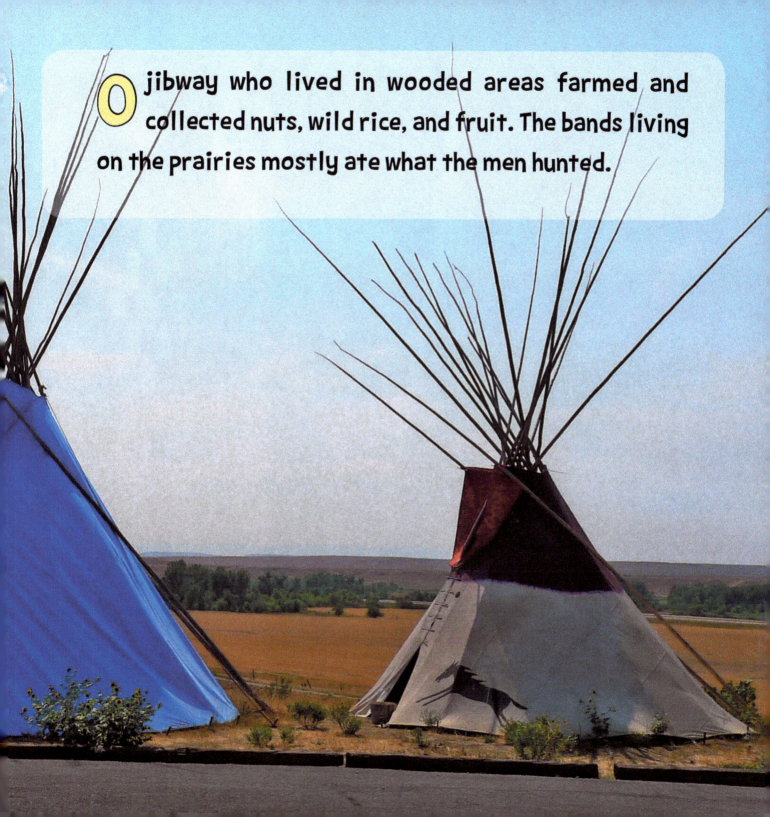

Ojibway who lived in wooded areas farmed and collected nuts, wild rice, and fruit. The bands living on the prairies mostly ate what the men hunted.

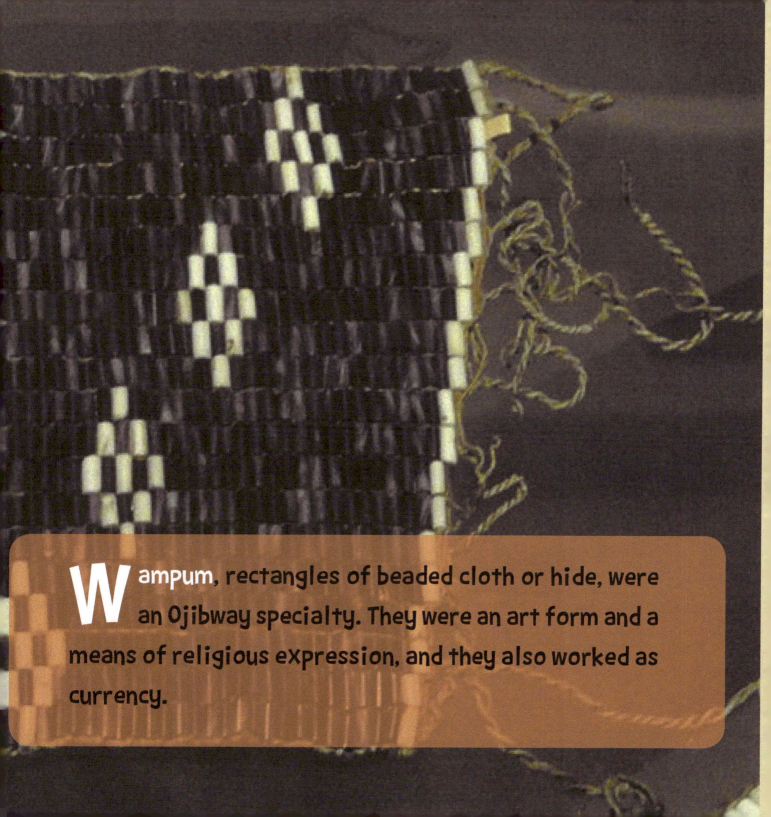

**W**ampum, rectangles of beaded cloth or hide, were an Ojibway specialty. They were an art form and a means of religious expression, and they also worked as currency.

# APACHE

The Apache people are a group of six tribes who share a comon culture and language. They lived in the American Southwest, and were connected with the Navajo people.

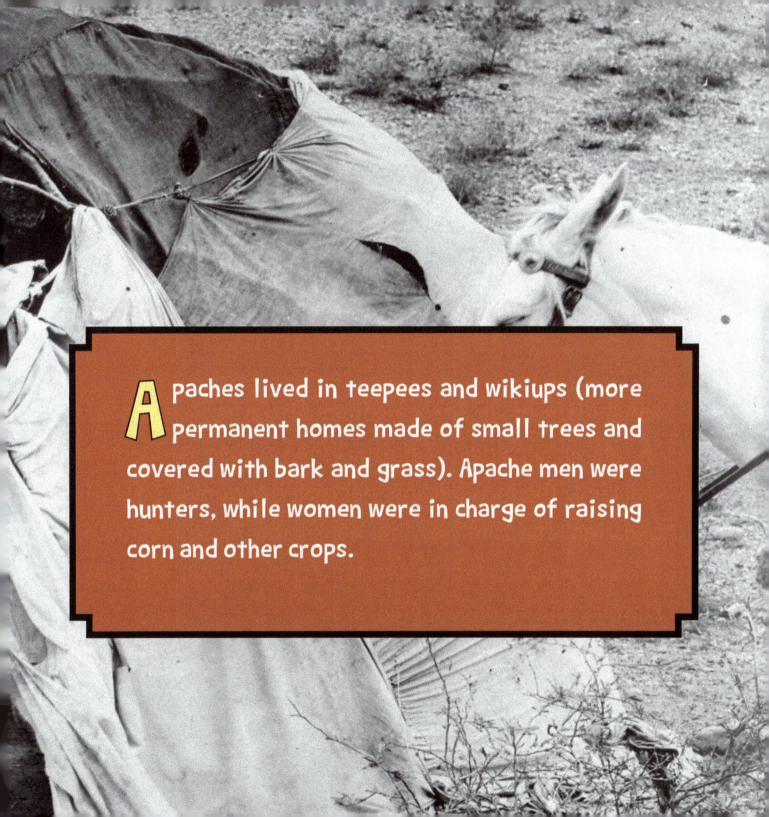

Apaches lived in teepees and wikiups (more permanent homes made of small trees and covered with bark and grass). Apache men were hunters, while women were in charge of raising corn and other crops.

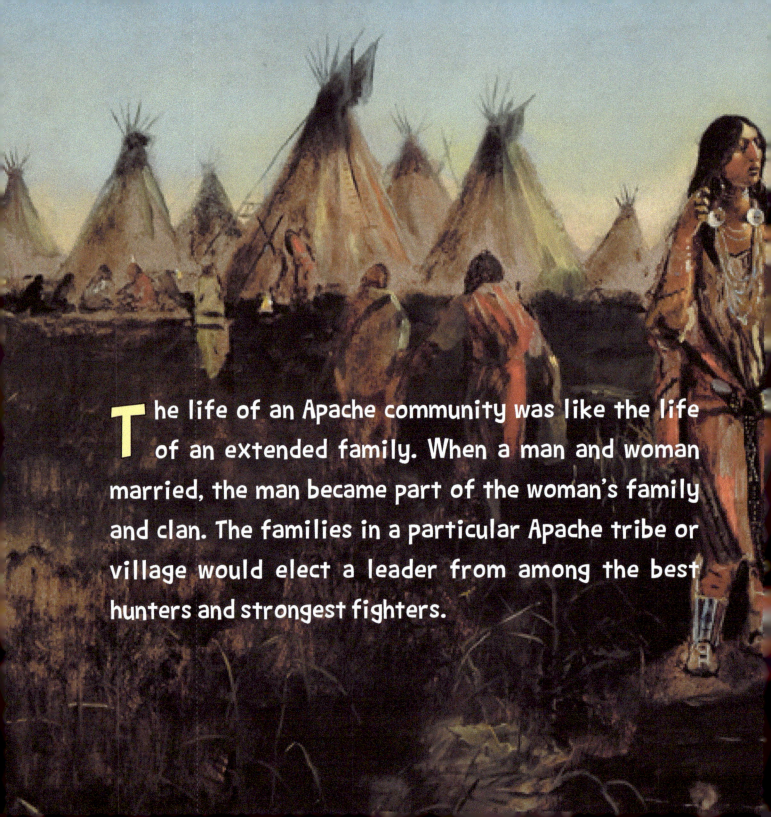

The life of an Apache community was like the life of an extended family. When a man and woman married, the man became part of the woman's family and clan. The families in a particular Apache tribe or village would elect a leader from among the best hunters and strongest fighters.

The Apaches fought hard against European settlers who were moving into their lands in the 1800s. They won many battles, but in the end the armies of the newcomers were too strong for the Apache fighters.

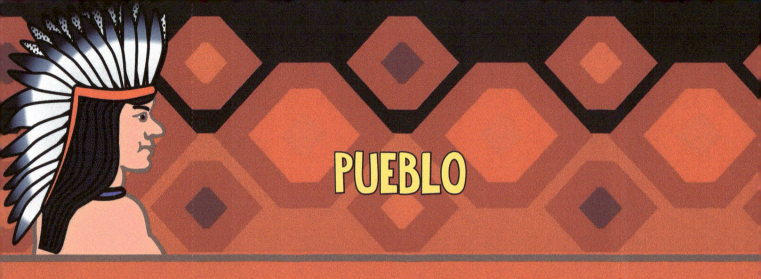

# PUEBLO

The Pueblo tribes live mainly in Arizona and New Mexico. They built villages of stone houses with mud walls, and when the Spanish arrived in the area in the 1500s, they found at least 70 Pueblo villages. Some Pueblo families still live in houses that are over a thousand years old!

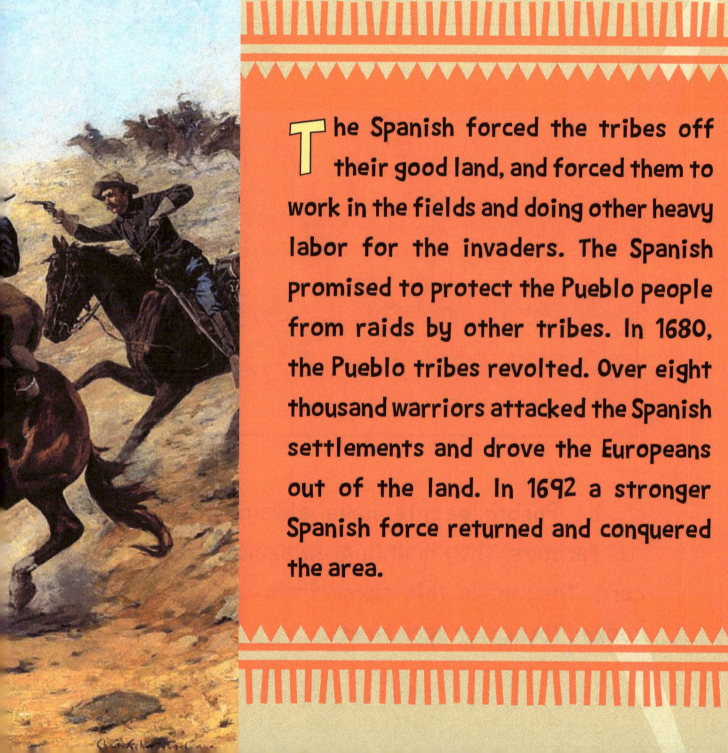

The Spanish forced the tribes off their good land, and forced them to work in the fields and doing other heavy labor for the invaders. The Spanish promised to protect the Pueblo people from raids by other tribes. In 1680, the Pueblo tribes revolted. Over eight thousand warriors attacked the Spanish settlements and drove the Europeans out of the land. In 1692 a stronger Spanish force returned and conquered the area.

## A CORN FARMER

The Pueblo people have always been great farmers. They mainly grew beans, squash, and corn. They made thin cakes from corn flour and cooked them over open fires.

Each Pueblo village had a "kiva", a special room in which Pueblo men carried out religious ceremonies. They had a strong mystical life, much of it involving spirits called "kachinas".

**IROQUOIS**

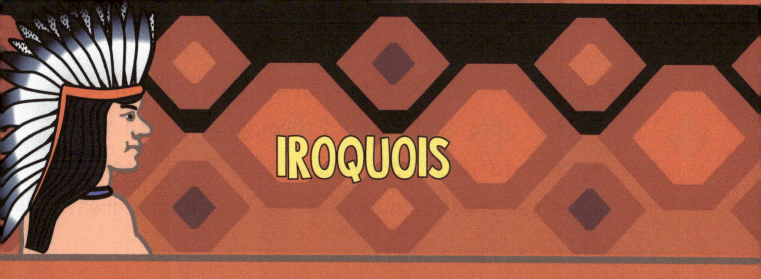

# IROQUOIS

The Iroquois Confederacy is six tribes in the northeast, in what is now New York, Ontario, Quebec, and Pennsylvania. Benjamin Franklin was so impressed by their form of government that he helped add some Iroquois ideas to the structure of government in the United States Constitution.

Each tribe was governed by an elected council, and the six tribes coordinated through a council that had representatives from every tribe. The women of the tribes selected the men who would go to the great council.

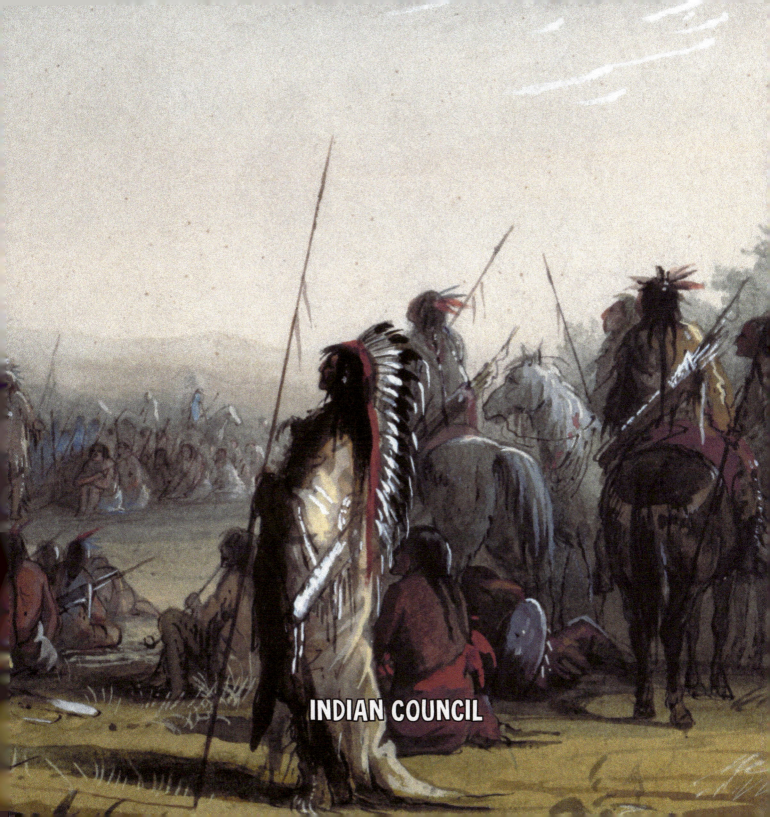

The tribes' name for themselves is "Haudenosaunee", which means "People of the Long House". Their houses were rectangles made of wood and covered with bark, sometimes over one hundred feet long. A village would be many longhouses surrounded by a defensive wooden wall.

Outside the wall, Iroquois villages had extensive fields for growing corn, beans, and squash. Women usually did the farming and food preparation, while men hunted for game ranging from turkey and rabbit to beaver and bear. Nobody ever went hungry as long as there was some food in the village to share.

# A STRUGGLE FOR A HOME

When the Europeans arrived in the New World, they thought they had discovered an empty paradise waiting to be settled and enjoyed. The Native Americans saw the land and the forests as their home and resisted attempts to push them out of their traditional areas. Read Baby Professor books like King Philip's War and The Wounded Knee Massacre to learn more about what happened when Native Americans resisted European settlement in the New World.

Milton Keynes UK
Ingram Content Group UK Ltd.
UKHW050921310824
447642UK00002B/65